forest hingeback tortoise

Those Terrific Turtles

Sarah Cussen

Illustrated by Steve Weaver

Photographs by David M. Dennis

Pineapple Press, Inc.
Sarasota, Florida

Inquiries should be addressed to:

Pineapple Press, Inc.
P.O. Box 3889
Sarasota, Florida 34230

www.pineapplepress.com

Library of Congress Cataloging-in-Publication Data

Cussen, Sarah, 1980-
Those terrific turtles / Sarah Cussen ; illustrated by Steve Weaver ; photographs by David M. Dennis. -- 1st ed.
p. cm.
Includes bibliographical references (p.   ) and index.
ISBN-13: 978-1-56164-363-9 (hardback : alk. paper)
ISBN-10: 1-56164-363-7 (hardback : alk. paper)
ISBN-13: 978-1-56164-364-6 (pbk. : alk. paper)
ISBN-10: 1-56164-364-5 (pbk. : alk. paper)
1.   Turtles--Juvenile literature.   I. Weaver, Steve, ill. II. Dennis, David M. III. Title.
QL666.C5C87 2006
597.92--dc22

2006008915

First Edition
Hb 10 9 8 7 6 5 4 3 2 1
Pb 10 9 8 7 6 5 4 3 2 1

Design by Steve Weaver
Printed in China

For Mom and Dad

Contents

An alligator snapper shows off his resemblance to a dinosaur.

How long have turtles been around?

When you see some kinds of turtles with their scaly heads and tails and bumps on their shells, you might think they look a little like dinosaurs. But actually turtles have lived on Earth even longer than the dinosaurs. They have been around 230 million years. That means they were here 50 million years before the first dinosaurs appeared.

A river terrapin, a turtle who likes to live near water,

and a Galápagos tortoise, who prefers the land.

What is the difference between a turtle and a tortoise?

Tortoises live their whole lives on land. They don't need to be near the water all the time. Turtles need to live in or near the water. The turtles you might find in your backyard or swimming in your pool are freshwater and wood turtles. Other turtles, called sea turtles, live their whole lives in the ocean. If you don't know whether to call it a turtle or a tortoise, you can use the scientific name for both—*Chelonia.*

A Florida softshell and a common map turtle show off the different types of shells a turtle can have.

What are turtle shells made of and why do they have them?

A turtle's top shell is called the carapace. Its bottom shell is called the plastron. These shells are actually made of bone—just like your skeleton. Turtle shells are covered with a type of scales, sort of like a fish. A turtle's shell is attached to its backbone and rib cage. So unlike in the cartoons, a turtle can't leave its shell. A turtle's shell gives it protection from predators and bad weather. A turtle's shell is very tough, but it is also sensitive to touch.

What is special about sea turtles?

Sea turtles spend almost their whole lives swimming in the ocean. They only come onto the land to lay eggs. What if you had to swim your whole life! They come up to breathe the air since they can't breathe under water like fish. They have flippers to help them swim. They are very good swimmers and can travel thousands of miles. Seven different kinds, or species, of sea turtles live in oceans all over the world.

1. leatherback
2. green
3. olive ridley
4. hawksbill
5. Kemp's ridley
6. loggerhead
7. flatback

The green sea turtle is an endangered species, mainly because people eat their meat and eggs.

Do people eat turtles?

Yes, some people hunt turtles for their meat and also collect their eggs to eat them. Certain kinds of turtles are very common and eating them is like eating any other fish or meat. Other kinds of turtles are rare and endangered. These turtles should never be harmed.
All of the different species of sea turtles are endangered.

Ceylon hill tortoise coming out of its egg.

Where do turtles lay their eggs?

Just like birds, turtles lay eggs. Some types of turtles lay one egg at a time and some lay hundreds. Can you imagine having a hundred brothers and sisters? Some types of turtles stay in their eggs for only about two months. Some types do not hatch for a whole year. All turtles and tortoises make nests by burying their eggs—in sand, in dirt, or under leaves.

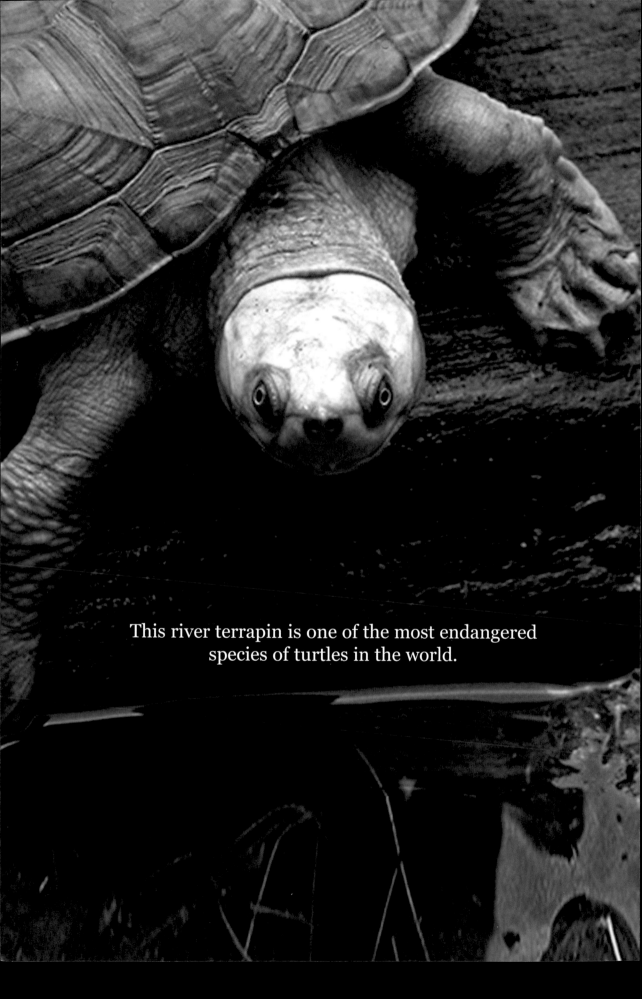

This river terrapin is one of the most endangered species of turtles in the world.

Why are some turtles endangered?

Turtles are endangered for the same reason most animals are—because of people. People gather the eggs of some types of turtles, so very few are born. People trap other types of turtles for their beautiful shells. In some parts of the world, people eat turtles. People build on land where turtles like to live, or hit them with their cars, or they poison turtles by accident with their garbage.

Many turtles are killed by getting caught in fishing lines or plastic bags. Also, there are more and more houses on the beaches where sea turtles need to build their nests.

This mother turtle has laid her eggs and is heading back to sea.

Why shouldn't I turn on lights on the beach at night?

Mother sea turtles crawl up onto beaches to dig a hole and lay their eggs. Then they return to the sea. When baby turtles come out of their eggs, they know to crawl toward the light of the moon reflected on the ocean. But they also crawl towards the lights on the porches of people who live on the beach. Then they get confused and never make it to the ocean. You can help baby turtles make it to the ocean by staying off the beach at night during the summer and keeping your porch lights off if you live by the beach.

The red-eared slider is a type of turtle some people keep as a pet.

Can I have a turtle as a pet?

Some people think that turtles should never be kept as pets because they need special care. But turtles have been popular pets for a long time. Turtles are hard to care for and very different from a cat or a dog. They are not good pets for kids since they need so much care but should not be touched. They need special large tanks, special food, and special lights. People often do not realize that small pet turtles can grow much bigger and live for a very long time.

This five-year-old girl shows you how big a Galapagos tortoise is.

How big are turtles?

Turtles come in many sizes. The biggest turtle overall is the leatherback sea turtle, which can grow to nearly 8 feet long and can weigh over 800 pounds. That's longer than the tallest basketball player and as heavy as a baby elephant. The largest tortoise is the Galapagos tortoise, which can grow over four feet long and weigh up to 660 pounds. That's about the weight of a pony. The smallest turtle is the bog turtle, which usually stays under four inches long. The smallest tortoise is the speckled cape padloper tortoise, which is under three inches long.

A Galapagos tortoise chows down on leaves.

What do turtles eat?

Most turtles are omnivores, which means that they eat both plants and animals. People are also omnivores. Turtles eat many different types of meat. They eat fish, snails, worms, and insects. Some turtles, though, are herbivores, or vegetarians. They eat only grasses, leaves, flowers, fruit, and even cactus. The leatherback and hawksbill sea turtles eat jellyfish, even poisonous ones. Other turtles have very powerful jaws so that they can crunch through the shells of food like clams or oysters.

A toad-headed
sideneck turtle.

How do turtles hide in their shells?

Only some types of turtles can pull their heads, legs, and feet inside their shells like in the cartoons. They are called "hidden-necked turtles" because they can hide their necks. In order to get inside their shells, some turtles have to blow the air out of their lungs, making a hissing sound. Some turtles have long necks and protect their heads by tucking them sideways up against their shell. They are called "side-necked turtles."

Would you want to stick your finger in this narrow-bridged mud turtle's mouth?

Are turtles dangerous to people?

There are no poisonous turtles. Turtles do not have teeth or fangs the way snakes do and they don't use venom. Turtles and other reptiles can carry germs that make people sick, so you should be careful. Wild turtles should not be touched, but if you ever touch a turtle, you should always wash your hands. Although they don't have teeth, turtles have very sharp jaws and might confuse your fingers for food!

You can see that this eastern box turtle has no ears, but maybe he is sniffing the air with his excellent nose.

Do turtles see, hear, or smell?

Turtles do not have ears on the outside of their heads like ours, but they can feel vibration and changes in the space around them so that they know where to find food or when to get away from another animal chasing them. Turtles do have excellent vision and see in color. They also have a very good sense of smell to help them find food. Sea turtles can even smell in water. If you've ever tried to sniff while you're in the pool, you know that all humans get is water up their noses!

Nobody has a face quite like this map turtle.

How can I tell two turtles apart?

As you have seen in this book, different species of turtles look very different. Some are big, some are small. Some have soft shells, some have hard shells. They are all different colors. But scientists who study turtles sometimes need to tell the differences between two turtles of the same species. This is tricky because in some types of turtles you can't even tell the difference between a boy and a girl just by looking. But the markings on the belly of a turtle's shell are always different. And the scales on a turtle's head are in a unique pattern. No two turtles are exactly alike.

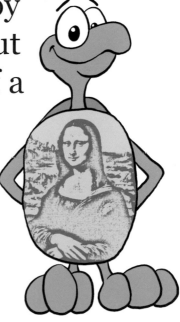

This Kemp's ridley sea turtle might be on its way to Mexico to lay its eggs.

How far can sea turtles travel?

Sea turtles spend their wholes lives in the sea, except to come ashore and lay their eggs. Imagine how far you could swim if you never got out of the water! Every year some loggerhead turtles swim all the way across the Atlantic Ocean. Kemp's ridley turtles stay mainly in the Gulf of Mexico, traveling between Mexico and Mississippi. Leatherbacks travel the farthest of all sea turtles. They have been found more than 3,000 miles from the beaches where they hatch!

This Galapagos tortoise even looks old.

How long do turtles live?

Some turtles can live a very long time. The large tortoises from the Galapagos Islands can live more than 200 years. Some sea turtles live 75 years or more. Even small pet turtles can live a long time. The red-eared slider is a common pet and can live up to 35 or 40 years if it receives proper care.

A peninsular cooter and a Florida redbellied turtle hang
out by the water.

Where do turtles live?

Turtles have been around for so long that they can be found everywhere on Earth except the Arctic and Antarctic. They have had a lot of time to adapt, or get used to, different environments. For example, most turtles have flippers so that they can swim. The turtles you are most likely to find live near fresh water, like ponds or rivers or lakes. But some tortoises are adapted to live in the desert. Some turtles live in the mountains. And sea turtles stay in the ocean almost all the time.

Florida or Bust!

This baby pancake tortoise knows where he's going.

Do turtles take care of their babies?

Mother turtles choose very carefully where to lay their eggs, looking for the safest place. You already learned that they dig a nest in the ground. When they get the nest just right, they bury the eggs. Most turtles leave the nests, but some turtles stay to make sure their eggs aren't eaten by snakes or other animals. But once the baby turtles have hatched, they are on their own. Unlike baby humans, turtles are born knowing how to take care of themselves.

SURVIVAL KIT

This African spurr thigh tortoise probably won't win any races.

Is it true that turtles are slow?

Actually, when they are in water, turtles can go pretty fast. The fastest turtle is the leatherback sea turtle, which has been clocked at 22 miles per hour! That's a lot faster than you can swim. But just as in the story "The Tortoise and the Hare," some species of tortoises are slowpokes. They walk only half a mile an hour. Try to walk in extreme slow motion and you'll see how slow they are.

Explore a Pond

Although you shouldn't bother a turtle living in a pond, a pond is still a great place to explore. You will discover all sorts of creatures besides turtles living there. You don't need special equipment to get a good look. You can make your own!

1. Tape a kitchen strainer to a long broom handle with duct tape to make a collecting net. You might catch water insects, tadpoles, crayfish, or snails. Never catch a turtle!

2. Make an observation pan out of the bottom of a gallon jug of milk. Ask someone to help you cut the bottom off the jug about three inches from the bottom. Fill it with clear pond water and add the creatures you caught. The top of the jug with the lid on makes a good collecting scoop in shallow water.

3. In your backpack, bring along a few plastic jars with lids that screw on (like clean peanut butter jars) to collect a few extra samples, a magnifying glass, and a field guide like *Pond Life* (A Golden Guide from St. Martin's Press) by George K. Reid.

Once you've finished taking a look, return everything to the pond. Remember—even the smallest bugs are an important part of life in the pond.

Make a Turtle Paperweight

You will need:
A styrofoam egg carton
Small pebbles
Small piece of cardboard
Popsicle sticks
Paint
Marker
Glue
Scissors

1. Cut one cup from an egg carton to make the turtle's shell. Fill the cup with small pebbles and glue a piece of cardboard on it to keep the pebbles inside. Trim the edges of the cardboard so it is the same size as the turtle's shell.

2. Cut off the rounded edges of the popsicle sticks to make the turtle's head and feet. Glue them to the cardboard. Draw eyes on the turtle's head.

3. Paint the turtle's shell.

Glossary

carapace – the top of a turtle's shell.

Chelonia – the scientific name for turtles and tortoises.

endangered – animals that are few in number and in danger of becoming extinct (dying off completely), usually due to their changing environment.

Galapagos Islands – islands in the Pacific Ocean along the equator known for their many interesting plants and animals, including giant tortoises.

herbivore – a vegetarian—or an animal that eats only plants.

omnivore – an animal that eats both plants and animals

plastron – the bottom of a turtle's shell.

predator – an animal that hunts other animals for food.

species – a particular kind of plant or animal.

venom – the poison used by animals to protect themselves or to hunt.

Where to Learn More about Turtles

Books Especially for Young Readers:

Ancona, George. *Turtle Watch*. New York: Macmillan Publishing Co., 1987.

Biel, Timothy Levi. *Zoobooks: Turtles*. Salem, Illinois: World Color, 1993.

Blassingame, Wyatt. *Wonders of the Turtle World*. New York: Dodd, Mead & Co., 1976.

Jacobs, Francine. *Sea Turtle: A Coloring Book in English and Spanish*. Washington, D.C.: Center for Environmental Education, 1981.

Other Books about Turtles:

Benton, Michael J., Ph.D. *The Reign of the Reptiles*. New York: Crescent Books, 1990.

Ernst, Carl H. and Robert W. Barbour. *Turtles of the World*. Washington, D.C.: Smithsonian Institution Press, 1989.

Obst, Fritz Jurgen. *Turtles, Tortoises and Terrapins*. New York: St. Martin's Press, 1986.

Websites:

http://www.turtles.org/kids.htm
A site about sea turtles for kids. Includes a webcam
to watch sea turtles live.

http://www.nationalgeographic.com/ngkids/9911/turtle/
A site for kids from National Geographic called "Turtles in Trouble."

About the Author

Sarah Cussen grew up in Sarasota, Florida, and now lives in Washington, D.C. She is also the author of *Those Peculiar Pelicans*. She is surrounded here by her nieces, Karina and Nadja Cussen, who helped her with the activities in this book.

Index

(Numbers in bold refer to photographs.)

If you enjoyed reading this book, here are some other Pineapple Press titles you might enjoy as well. To request our complete catalog or to place an order, write to Pineapple Press, P.O. Box 3889, Sarasota, Florida 34230, or call 1-800-PINEAPL (746-3275). Or visit our website at www.pineapplepress.com.

Those Amazing Alligators by Kathy Feeney. Illustrated by Steve Weaver. Alligators are amazing animals, as you'll see in this book. Discover the differences between alligators and crocodiles; learn what alligators eat, how they communicate, and much more. Ages 5–9.

Those Outrageous Owls by Laura Wyatt. Illustrated by Steve Weaver, photographs by H. G. Moore III. Learn what owls eat, how they hunt, and why they look the way they do. You'll find out what an owlet looks like, why horned owls have horns, and much more! Ages 5–9.

Those Excellent Eagles by Jan Lee Wicker. Illustrated by Steve Weaver, photographs by H.G. Moore III. Learn all about those excellent eagles—what they eat, how fast they fly, why the American Bald Eagle is our nation's national bird. You'll even make some edible eagles! Ages 5–9.

Those Peculiar Pelicans by Sarah Cussen. Illustrated by Steve Weaver, photographs by Roger Hammond. Find out how much food those peculiar pelicans can fit in their beaks, how they stay cool, whether they really steal fish from fishermen. And learn how to fold up an origami pelican. Ages 5–9.

Those Funny Flamingos by Jan Lee Wicker. Illustrated by Steve Weaver. Flamingos are indeed funny birds. Learn why those funny flamingos are pink, stand on one leg, eat upside down, and much more. Ages 5–9.

Drawing Florida Wildlife by Frank Lohan. The clearest, easiest method yet for learning to draw Florida's birds, reptiles, amphibians, and mammals. All ages.

Dinosaurs of the South by Judy Cutchins and Ginny Johnston. Dinosaurs lived in the southeastern United States. Loaded with full-color fossil photos as well as art to show what the dinos might have looked like. Ages 8–12.

Ice Age Giants of the South by Judy Cutchins and Ginny Johnston. Learn about the huge animals and reptiles that lived here during the Ice Age. Meet saber-toothed cats, dire wolves, mammoths, giant sloths, and more. Ages 8–12.

Giant Predators of the Ancient Seas by Judy Cutchins and Ginny Johnston. Meet the giant creatures that prowled the waters of prehistory. Ages 8–12.

Florida A to Z by Susan Jane Ryan. Illustrated by Carol Tornatore. From Alligator to Zephyrhills, you'll find out more about Florida packed in this alphabet than you can imagine—200 facts and pictures on Florida history, geography, nature, and people. Ages 8–12.

Florida Lighthouses for Kids by Elinor De Wire. Learn why some lighthouses are tall and some short, why a cat parachuted off St. Augustine Lighthouse, where Florida skeleton and spider lighthouses stand, and much more. Lots of color pictures. Ages 9 and up.